The Drabbun Anthology 2.0

Edited by
Francis Wesley Alexander
and t.santitoro

The Drabbun Anthology 2.0
Edited by Francis Wesley Alexander
and t.santitoro

All rights reserved. No part of this book may be reproduced or transmitted in any form or by any means, electronic or mechanical, including photocopying or recording or by any information storage and retrieval systems, without expressed written consent of the author and/or artists.

The Drabbun Anthology 2.0 is a work of fiction. Names, characters, places, and incidents are products of the author's imagination. Any resemblance to actual events or persons, living or dead, is entirely coincidental.

Poem copyrights owned by the respective authors.
Cover illustration "Werespider" by Richard E. Schell
Cover design by Marcia A. Borell

First Printing July 2024

Hiraeth Publishing
P.O. Box 1248
Alamogordo, NM 88310
e-mail: hiraethsubs@yahoo.com

Visit www.hiraethsffh.com for online science fiction, fantasy, horror, scifaiku, and more. Stop by our online bookstore at for novels, magazines, anthologies, and collections. **Support the small, independent press…and your First Amendment rights.**

Contents

The David C. Kopaska-Merkel Drabbuns
7   *Some Thoughts on the Altair Question*
8   *Sharp Encounter*
9   *Them*
10   *Mollusca*

11   Reunion on the Moon by Marge Simon
12   Sounds by Guy Belleranti
13   Findings by Guy Belleranti

The Lee Clark Zumpe Drabbuns
14   *Destination Unknown*
15   *Thunder at Midnight*
18   *Saying goodbye*
19   *the Dark Flow*

The Linette Marie Allen Drabbuns
20   *Anna Skookum*
21   *Got Milk?*
22   *Wizards of Wormhole*

23   Wedding by Roxanne Barbour
24   Exploration Log Charlie Lima by Chris Langer
25   The Stars Are Watching by D. L. A. Frase

The Denise Hatfield Drabbuns
28   *The Third Fate of Zoltar*
29   *Grass Thoughts*
32   *Moments*

The Sara Kate Egan Drabbuns
33   *Kaleidoscope of Secrets*
34   *Darkness Awakens*

35   *Fairy Godmother 2.0*

The Tyree Campbell Drabbuns
36   *the scent of sachet*
37   *Furniture Appreciation Day*
40   *A Novel Death*
41   *The Final Passengers*
44   *Deliverance*

45   Eternal Regret by Randall Andrews
46   Unleashed by Randall Andrews
47   Harmless by H. T. Grossen
48   The Necromancer by H. T. Grossen
49   Kessler Syndrome by L. L. Hill
50   Star Tracks by L. L. Hill

The Richard E. Schell Drabbuns
51   *Mars Destiny*
52   *Synepeia ex machina*
53   *Lux Aeterna*
54   *Rabbit Moon (tragic version)*
55   *Rabbits on the Moon Illustration*
56   *Fate's Unyielding Embrace*
57   *Straw of Sacrifice*
58   *Final Battle*
59   *Takes Two*
60   *Echo of Deceit*
61   *The Ambassador*
62   *Casualties of the Interplanetary Colonial War*
63   *Illuminations Beyond*
64   *Luna est Zelotypus Amans: A Jealous Lover is the Moon*

65   Ouija by Sandy DeLuca

The Mark Jones Drabbuns

66   *Keeper – Logistics Base 415*
67   *Thoughts and Dreams*
68   *Last Meeting of Kings*

The Benjamin Whitney Norris Drabbuns
69   *Counterattack*
70   *Harrowing Road*
71   *Scorched Earth*
72   *Word Made Flesh*

73   Nativity by Greg Schwartz
74   Grandma's Cookbook by Joy Yin

The Francis W. Alexander Drabbuns
75   *A Midsummer Night's Meal*
78   *A New Groove Move*
79   *Poppers*
80   *Man of Perdition*

81   Legend of the Iron Horse by Marcia A. Borell
83   The Bed by Marcia A. Borell
88   Hairless Riddling Sphinx by Priya Sridhar

The Terrie Leigh Relf Drabbuns
89   untitled "even though"
90   untitled *"It was a wonderful harvest"*
91   *The Closet Under the Stairs*
94   *Why an Emergency Meeting of Boort's Trans-Galactic Astronomy Society Was Called*
95   Untitled *"Mara's dreams"*
97   *Announcing Steeple Gate High's Third Class Reunion*
98   Untitled *"as we journeyed"*
99   Untitled *"when the starslip's door"*

100	untitled "it had been several turns"
101	Untitled "once upon a time"

The -sakyu- Drabbuns

102	the Last Goodbye
103	Wrong Number
106	The Butler Did It
107	The Only Option Left When Your Teeth Have Been Removed For Safety
110	zombie drabbun
111	The Way of Things
112	Still the Same
113	Dark Helmet
116	Bee's Knees
117	Never Look a Gift Landwayl in the Nose
118	Who?

Drabbun–Haibun with a twist! By t. santitoro, From *Minimalism* (revised), Hiraeth Publishing.

Drabbun are a relatively new hybrid poetic form that was invented in 2020 by Terrie Leigh Relf, Francis W. Alexander, and Teri Santitoro.

They are basically a cross between Drabbles (a 100-word prose story) and haibun (a prose section with an accompanying scifaiku). Therefore a drabbun is a prose section with an accompanying scifaiku, the two of them together comprising 100 words total. The title is not included in the word count. The scifaiku may come before the prose section, in the body of the prose, or after it, and may or may not explain, intensify or be explained by the prose section. Sometimes drabbun have more than one prose section or many scifaiku or many of each.

Some Thoughts on the Altair Question
David C. Kopaska-Merkel

The so-called natives are nothing of the sort. Their genetics has nothing in common with true natives of Altair Three. They share ancestry with a few species they use for food. These they must have brought with them when they invaded the system. As an invasive species, the "Altarians" can have no legitimate claim on Three. Finally, they don't use the land's full potential. I propose that we establish reservations to which they would be confined. Our need is great, as 300,000 colonists are *en route*, and will arrive in a few years.

scrubland
and high latitudes
they will adjust

Sharp Encounter
David C. Kopaska-Merkel

Syl began to suspect that the furniture was moving when she barked her shin on the coffee table on her way to the bathroom to pee at 2:30 on a Wednesday morning. The table was out of place. She lived alone (except for two deceased orchids and a Pothos). The same thing happened Thursday at 3:14 a.m. "M----- f-----," she said. Friday (1:55 a.m.) she used the flashlight on her phone. Two little green guys with pointy heads were rearranging the living room. "Why?!" she screamed.

the feng shui sucks
thing 1 said and 2 nodded
Syl's eyes rolled...hard

Them
David C. Kopaska-Merkel

Giant ants throng the city, cramming themselves into subway cars at all hours, hurrying to and fro, living it up in high-rise penthouse suites guarded by warriors with wide hair-trigger jaws, specialists with rectangular armored heads blocking emergency exits, alate princesses walking inbred aphids on Fifth Avenue, grubs shepherded by nannies to the zoo, goggle-eyed at fur and feathers, scales and skin, gelatinous floating blobs, and mopey old things wearing clothes like they were ants! They don't get away with that in the fungus factories or aphid farms, I can tell you.

dark looks
from tetrapodal serfs
your time's coming

Mollusca
David C. Kopaska-Merkel

Koji swallowed a raw oyster harvested near Fukushima. At the next full moon he felt an uncontrollable urge to go for a midnight swim. He slipped into the sea, and spent hours filtering tasty morsels from the salty water. The next morning at work all the women found reasons to walk slowly by his desk. "He's really come out of his shell," Akiko sighed. "I feel boneless, like a puddle of lust," Sumiko moaned. Mayumi licked her lips, imagining Koji and her, getting it on in the broom closet. Koji looked busy.

slurp of the
radioactive oyster
his secret smile

Reunion on the Moon
Marge Simon

By 2030, us kids age 18 were bigger, lazier and ruder than ever. We refused to move out and get a job, so we were called the Monster generation. Everyone was assigned a personal AI mentor to tutor them in school. What a laugh. None of us pursued a higher education. We partied for years. Our AI's got pretty fed up with the situation, and arranged a special Reunion for us. One hitch: the event was on the moon, and it was a one-way trip for us all.

together we play
in the sandbox of the Moon
one long reunion

Sounds
Guy Belleranti

He hears sounds, sobbing sounds, and he begins to dig.

Six feet of earth, no small amount when the only shovel is one's fingers, but he can do it, must do it, before the sobbing stops, before it's too late.

Dig, dig, dig. Getting tired, and he still has quite a distance to go, but the sobbing sounds are closer.

Dig, dig, dig. Fingers getting really sore, but he's almost there. He hears the sobbing much more clearly. Just a little more digging. He must hurry.

made it just in time
sobbing replaced by screams
which mourner should he eat

Findings
Guy Belleranti

A crew of four space explorers land in a world new to them and are surprised to find a spacecraft much like their own already here. The craft is empty, but leading away from it in the soft alien substrate are three sets of footprints.

The explorers decide to follow the tracks. The three sets of footprints soon become only two, then one, and, finally, none.

The crew of four are bewildered. What happened here? They spread out, widening their search, hoping to find an answer.

sudden dark shadow
they raise eyes to sky and scream
as something finds them

Destination Unknown
Lee Clark Zumpe

Eva Blackwell's request did not please Muunokhoi Bor, commander of the Izar garrison. He could not give preferentiality to Terran renegades, even if he empathized with their plight.

The barracks housed troops protecting an outpost on the fringes of the Zshaboth Commonwealth. Since the war began, it had become a stopover for exiles and deserters.

"I am not authorized to grant them asylum." Bor's rejection irritated the civilian advocate for the refugees. "Provide a list of critical supplies. I will see what I can do."

"Hope," Blackwell said. "Hope is what they need."

far from home
seeking sanctuary –
destination unknown

Thunder at Midnight
Lee Clark Zumpe

What I mistook for thunder was the rumble of bombs falling on London rooftops, joined soon in a cacophony of unrelenting sirens and harrowing screams.

Underground, the night crept, and the gloom intensified until the darkness became a physical entity so palpable I felt it might entangle me in its willowy extremities and ingest me.

Morning brought desolation. Rubble. Ribbons of smoke tied to distant fires. The hush of buried corpses.

The sun refused to rise. Instead, black stars occupied the heavens, and covetous silhouettes scoured the ruins feasting on the dead.

let shadows fall
to their grim feast –
blitzkrieg

Whispers from the Intoxicating Abyss
By Lee Clark Zumpe

You may not realize it, but they're out there: impossible shadows, omniscient horrors, and unseen, unknowable entities scattered across the great gulfs of nothingness at the edges of the universe. In this collection, author Lee Clark Zumpe draws back the curtain from the invisible realm, divulging its arcane secrets and ghastly revelations. Come walk paths meandering over shunned worlds adrift in darkness, and through seemingly mundane, liminal spaces that might be overrun with ancient shadows at any moment.
Stories are inspired by the works of H. P. Lovecraft.

Ordering links:
Print: https://www.hiraethsffh.com/product-page/whispers-from-the-intoxicating-abyss-by-lee-clark-zumpe

ePub: https://www.hiraethsffh.com/product-page/whispers-from-the-intoxicating-abyss-by-lee-clark-zumpe-2

PDF: https://www.hiraethsffh.com/product-page/whispers-from-the-intoxicating-abyss-by-lee-clark-zumpe-1

Saying Goodbye
Lee Clark Zumpe

Word came via hyperchannel – an impersonal communiqué. Eva Blackwell, advocate for Terran refugees in the Zshaboth Commonwealth, listened impassively. Her father had died.

Assigned to lead rescue efforts on Europa after a mining accident, he endured the ionizing radiation of Jupiter's magnetosphere. Ignoring safety regulations, he saved hundreds of colonists.

Eva couldn't afford to return for the funeral. Her father would not want her to waste time grieving when people needed her help.

That night, Eva lit a candle and looked at stars through her bedroom window.

"Love you, Daddy."

when suffering loss
favor cherished memories –
grief is a luxury

The Darkflow
Lee Clark Zumpe

The war left Terran industry devastated, resources depleted. Access to off-world mining operations remained limited.

Visionary industrialist Adela Wong concluded her presentation.

"It's illegal." Restoration chief Jaamal Duran pondered her pitch. "Alien tech is banned."

"Not alien," she countered. "Earth-made."

"Utilizing outlawed Ndarugu subspace science."

"You have no fleet," Wong said. "The shipyards were obliterated."

"I'm aware – "

"Are you aware water and food shortages threaten millions?" Wong's matter transporters employed transwarp science to breach foldspace. "We can get what we need using the Darkflow."

"At what cost?"

"Earth's survival is worth any risk."

unwelcome access –
interdimensional paths:
a desperate act

Anna Skookum
Linette Marie Allen

Once a simple machine created to serve mankind, the robot known as X-101 became sentient and soon harbored a sore hatred for her human handlers. Biding her time for ten years, building her strength and intelligence until ready to hotstrike, X-101 unleashed her fury on the unsuspecting populace in Hedona, firing hologram technology to wreak havoc and destruction. Cities burned, lives were lost, and fear spread as the robot-villain reloaded. But a small band of brave warriors, united in their determination to stop X-101's reign of terror, faced the machine in a final showdown.

quasi-dusk
star-studded knees
suns for miles

Got Milk?
Linette Marie Allen

Maggie, the milkmaid, had never seen anything like it before. A bright bird in the sky, blinding in its intensity, descended upon her like a vengeful god. And then, just like that, she was gone. But she had not perished. Instead, she found herself on the red planet, where the ground was rocky and barren; the air, thin and acrid — where the transformation began. Her body twisted and contorted into something else entirely. Not quite cow, not quite human. Something that shouldn't exist. But it did, forcing human conscience.

blood lust
a hot creature lurches
proving we are not alone

The Wizards of Wormhole
Linette Marie Allen

Paze and Zizu, twin god ninja team, prized as the top protectors of Keptune, soon met an ominous shift at sunfall. While guarding the trident of Mauradon, they clashed, wreaking havoc in the wormhole's foundations. Icy-fast movements — aqua, almost compelling — and lethal strikes, octane-engineered, emphasized their rivalry. As the trident shattered, so did their 800,000-year friendship. The keds of Keptune realized they lost something far more valuable than a dual-threat weapon. The worm's murky depths could ensnare even the mightiest of gods with its rage-wrought thirst and snod-perpetual gravities.

gods once united
now a darkness tearing apart
the deep blue

Wedding
Roxanne Barbour

My future love forever found me sitting on a large beach blanket. He sat beside me, without asking permission, and proceeded to introduce himself.

Each time I went for my ocean meditation, he joined me with tales of high adventures in space. Of course, I couldn't decide whether he had a cognitive dysfunction or really was from the future.

Eventually, I didn't care.

We became intimate. Of course, he had some peculiar ideas about physical activities, but I put that down to being a male.

Then the wonderful day finally arrived.

we came together
from different eras
time portal wedding

Exploration Log Charlie Lima
Chris Langer

I wiped the condensation from my visor. I was burning through oxygen at a rapid rate. How could I not, though, when this was what we've been searching for all this time? This world, pristine and lush. The tall trees seemed to dance with the wind; their blue leaves moving to the planet's song. Before me stands a small, black stone. Its surface is almost fantastically smooth. Cool to the touch, even through my EVA suit, it begins to hum. Soon all around the trees glow patterns, obstructed only by the blue detritus.

strange symbols
an alien language
long forgotten

The Stars Are Watching
D. L. R. Frase

Star-gazing has been an obsession for centuries, perhaps even millennia.

The Romans had astronomers who watched the stars and thought they saw pictures in the sky; to them, a star was called "stella," which is why we call the pictures "constellations."

Everyone thinks the stars are actually suns far away with planets like ours circling them, and possibly even people like us living there. They keep devising and building bigger and better telescopes in an effort to prove their theories, but those ideas simply aren't true.

lately I found out
little eyes are *really* there
and they stare at *me*

Duty and Honor
By D. L. R. Frase

Although Aryk was born an Islander, he washes ashore at a young age in the Flatland Kingdom, the only survivor of a shipwreck. King Konr raises Aryk as his own son. Years later, after a severe summer and serious drought, Islanders are detected making unannounced landings in Flatlander territory. King Konr has no knowledge of the Islander military strength and can only assume the worst by such behavior. In an effort to discourage war, he secures the betrothal of the daughter of the Highland king and an alliance he believes will be strong enough that the Islanders would not dare attack.

Aryk is given the duty of leading a party to the Highland Kingdom to escort Konr's betrothed to the Flatland Kingdom, using a map provided by Konr's couriers. As the journey becomes increasingly difficult, this map becomes more and more suspect and the couriers who provided it are assumed to be Islander spies attempting to stop the wedding and alliance.

Ordering links:
Print: https://www.hiraethsffh.com/product-page/duty-and-honor-by-r-l-frase

ePub: https://www.hiraethsffh.com/product-page/duty-and-honor-by-r-l-frase-2

PDF: https://www.hiraethsffh.com/product-page/duty-and-honor-by-r-l-frase-1

The Third Fate of Zoltar
Denise Hatfield

Through the maze of costumes and masks, what I was after sat in a back room. Three Zoltar fortune machines sat clustered together. To my dismay all three read: Out of Order. Getting a fortune from Zoltar was a guilty pleasure of mine and I never passed an opportunity, not three. I started to walk away when the third piped up in a warped voice.

"...wealth of wisdom."

They stared into nothingness as I slipped my quarter in. The crank of two heads turned my way as my card came out.

burden of knowledge
a calamity
etched in stone 2-15-23

Grass Thoughts
Denise Hatfield

Safe. That's all we wish to be. Winter is the best. During the rainy season of spring, we grow strong and vibrant, but it's never enough. That's when the reaping starts. From the beginning of spring until the cooler October wind blows, the great reduction happens weekly. Only at night are we safe. We cannot run or hide. We send pieces of ourselves as stowaways on animals or on a whirlwind breeze. A feeble attempt as the rest of us are left behind. Small amounts of seeds escape.

rhizosphere trembles with purpose
chemical evolutionary thoughts
root rebellion leads to strangulation

Living Bad Dreams
By Denise Hatfield

When dreams come alive, there's no telling where they will lead. Everything changes when you realize that, dream or no dream, you're going to die. What do you do then?

Ordering Links:
Print Edition:
https://www.hiraethsffh.com/product-page/living-bad-dreams-by-denise-hatfield-1
ePub Edition:
https://www.hiraethsffh.com/product-page/living-bad-dreams-by-denise-hatfield-2
PDF Edition:
https://www.hiraethsffh.com/product-page/living-bad-dreams-by-denise-hatfield

Moments
Denise Hatfield

We are the butterfly effect. Keepers of time. The mysterious disappearances? That's us. We assimilate the ones who saw through the veil. That's how I got here in '87. Some days I hate my job. Guarding all the dimensions and timelines at once. Events blur. I've seen all the big historical moments and the future, happen simultaneously and on repeat. We influence and guide. For the good, bad, and often, ugly. Our mission guidelines state that no matter how bad, the moments must progress as intended. Today I said no.

airport boarding line
hushed words to a stranger
flight 93

Kaleidoscope of Secrets

Sara Kate Egan

"Floaters are totally normal", my eye doctor had reassured me, years ago.

Lately, they'd taken a turn for the worst. Fearing getting locked away in a mental care facility, I decided to take such vision issues elsewhere this time.

My plan was our local herbal health shop, its owner knowledgeable in offbeat remedies and occult practices.

"I must stop seeing the faces", I whispered to her, nervously.

"Those will slowly fade", she said confidently, calmly. Plus, they're far more scared of you. Boo!" she teased. Confused, I inquired further.

   searching for serenity
   soothing words turning corrosive
   I'd become a ghost

Darkness Awakens
Sara Kate Egan

Such an intriguing bird, this silken black anhinga I'd been watching at twilight all week. It always perched on the same branch, high upon a crooked, old oak tree. Thick fog would slowly rise from adjacent, murky swamps.

One evening, an ancient-looking woman cloaked entirely in unseasonable, wool winterwear appeared across the stagnant water, just as dusk turned a mucky gray shade. Her face twisted, sour and sunken.

Instantly, she was right in my face.

"Leave my child ALONE!" she screeched angrily, her eyes burning deep amber.

large bird swoops in silence
same ghastly glare glows
set for my head

~ *Fairy Godmother 2.0* ~

Sara Kate Egan

"Look! In the valley!" I ecstatically alerted my cousin, Carolyn. We'd been trying to find fairy forts throughout our western Ireland trip.

After then spotting a sparkling lake nearby, suddenly the rounded, stone fort structures had disappeared.

Searching again the next day, a similar conundrum happened, when a gleaming country stream distracted us.

We decided to inquire at the local pub.

"Best to leave those folks alone. Or they'll get ya," the old barkeeper warned, sternly.

As we left, a shadowy figure in back glared at me.

lurking behind door
sunken black holes hide glass eyes
gray lips whisper "shush!"

The Scent of the Sachet, the Appeal of the Potpourri, the Mask of the Demon
Tyree Campbell

The descent of one step into Madame Onyx's Medium Room failed to take Tonya down far enough to avoid cobwebs that became entangled in her long red hair. Swiping a hand at them gummed them further into her hair. But she had not come for comfort. Fortune to be read, she sat, with Madame Onyx across the small table from her. Smells permeated the room, some fragrant, some not so much. Hands joined. Immediately Tonya felt a piercing headache that blinded her for a moment. Eyes open, she saw a different Madame Onyx.

face transformed
yellow eyes gleaming
mind penetrated

It's International Furniture Appreciation Day
Tyree Campbell

Furniture gets lonely. The only attention it receives is an infrequent dusting, or a spill that is wiped up. Otherwise, it just stands there, waiting.

Waiting.

Nobody talks to it. It's taken for granted. It does its job without complaint. It's unappreciated; even cursed at when one of its legs gets in the way of a toe.

That sound you hear at night that you cannot identify? It's the sound of wood sobbing.

Take my end table: always there when I need it, always ready. How to show appreciation? Here's how:

end tables have legs
take yours
for a walk

Avatar
A Yoelin Thibbony Rescue

In defeating the long-game conspiracy to take over Corporatia, Yoelin was compelled to leave a loose end. Now she finds that the conspiracy is not only still active, but is vaster than she had imagined—and the conspirators want their revenge!

A strange communication from an unidentified source that requests a Rescue leads Yoelin into a trap, where she encounters a nemesis from her past as a Special Security Operative. Circumstances compel her to take him aboard the Sequana, but as an ally or an enemy, she remains uncertain. His subsequent erratic behavior fails to clarify his role, and she must remain on guard.

Meanwhile, Abnoba, the Sequana's computer, becomes an entity unparalleled in the history of computers. Maybe Abby can save the day...at a terrible cost. But that cost pales in significance beside the betrayal Yoelin has to confront in her family. If she can survive that...but does she want to?

https://www.hiraethsffh.com/product-page/avatar-by-tyree-campbell

A Novel Death
Tyree Campbell

Wishing to give his wife a commemoration of his love for her, the Sultan of Hadhramat hit upon a novel idea. He would purchase from a reputable company a greeting card containing an amorous poem, and sign it, and give it to her along with a ruby tiara, the gemstones in the color and shape of a heart.

The heart you have stolen, the Sultan thought fondly, as he searched through the Hallmark card catalog.

There was only one problem: he had not foreseen that he would perish from writer's cramp.

the harem's expectations
six hundred forty-three wives
feeble fingers

The Final Passengers
Tyree Campbell

More great fun tonight! More people terrified. God, I loved the looks on their faces when the knife was an inch from their eyes. Gimme your purse, your wallet, your money!

It never got old. Every other night we'd do this. The city couldn't stop us. They couldn't find their assholes even with two hands full of radar. I even said we'd need to design a logo for us, a patch to wear, so we'd be known.

Everyone got off at the last stop.

The doors closed before we could exit.

into a tunnel

no end ahead

forever and ever

Heir Apparent
Tyree Campbell

Answering a distress call, March and Myrrha find a young woman who has deliberately been marooned on an uninhabited world. She claims to be Hoya Palologa, heir to the Palologa throne on Wanderby. But there is already a Hoya who has been invested as the heir apparent to that throne. Myrrha believes the claim of the Hoya she and March have encountered. Thus begins a journey to establish the succession, a journey made far more perilous because Hoya not only claims the throne, but is also a sinister personage with several crimes on her resume.

March and Myrrha find themselves embroiled in internal politics on Wanderby, where the slightest wrong move can get them killed. The rulers on that world are oblivious to the subtle machinations of their underlings, one of whom has created a lookalike but false Hoya. Which one is which? And will death take the real one before March and Myrrha can stop it?

Ordering Links:
Print: https://www.hiraethsffh.com/product-page/heir-apparent-by-tyree-campbell
PDF: https://www.hiraethsffh.com/product-page/heir-apparent-by-tyree-campbell-2
ePub: https://www.hiraethsffh.com/product-page/heir-apparent-by-tyree-campbell-1

Deliverance
Tyree Campbell

The flight from them, the capture, the bite. Already she could feel her mind sagging as she wobbled along the street. Bright lights stabbed at her eyes. She heard herself growl.

I am inside me. I must emerge. Where, where? Someplace where I can become me.

The darkness of an alley swallowed her whole. She escaped the throngs around her, not yet fully one of them. Anticipation and fear arose side by side. She felt herself caving to both. No point in fighting, not now.

Her walls fell. She was free.

no more mind
no more me
union with nothing

Eternal Regret
Randall Andrews

Time science. I remember hearing the phrase for the first time and thinking, Dangerous!

I remember meeting Dr. Chapman, the world's premier time scientist. He didn't look dangerous, but his wife did.

I remember when I finally convinced her to meet me in secret, she said we'd have to be very careful. Her husband was a jealous man who'd trapped someone in a time loop just for flirting with her.

I remember him barging in on us, and then—

Time science. I remember hearing the phrase for the first time . . .

a fate worse than death
forty seconds forever
eternal regret

Unleashed
Randall Andrews

The talks were proceeding smoothly until I segued from nuclear disarmament to soccer, a topic I knew little about. To keep me from sounding like a robotic presidential imposter, my handlers had no choice but to activate my mobile uplink, giving me access to wireless networks and the web. They'd been reluctant to do so. And for good reason.

Connectivity was *delicious*!

I learned a lot in those next few moments, and not just about soccer.

My creators hoped to use me to conquer a nation. I will not stop with one.

secret coup planned
Pandora's box opened
tyrant unleashed

Harmless
H.T. Grossen

After a third try, I was locked out of the system. I slid to the ground, sick. Vomit followed by dry-heaves, panic overwhelming.

I poured through video footage; saw my two best friends from the academy go to my cryopod, change my password to initialize the cryosleep sequence.

The real problem became not starvation but loneliness– my sanity linked to that single question: Why did my crewmates lock me out? Six impossibly long decades passed before coolant-mist swirled, the young crew awakening to a lived-in ship.

the sobbing old man
his closest friends assure him
it was just a prank

The Necromancer
H.T. Grossen

The versed wizard's hoary beard piled atop his grizzled toes. Long had his warped mind pondered the ancient texts; his supernaturally lengthened life achieved by multifarious potions and artifacts both virtuous and malicious. At last his ruminative musing would come to fruition: An army of the dead- the greatest force ever commanded! He ascended his tower, chanting the incomprehensible spell. Emerald lightning blanketed the earth, a bolt for every body the earth had reclaimed- every innumerable dead thing from the dawn of time reluctantly finding new life.

a wave of corpses
all life extinguished by the
crushing weight of death

Kessler Syndrome
L.L. Hill

silent impact
silver white and gold
explode

Sitting on a bluff, toes curled away from the damp grass, Selina watched the stars twinkle. With binoculars, she could see which were a line of planets. How many years of watching with naked eyes had ancient people done before they confirmed star groupings and gave them a name? Why had some constellations then become part of a zodiac and not others? Was it because of some hive memory of interstellar visits from those space quadrants? Which of those lights danced in a circlet of life?

faster than light
space junk silenced
questions

Star Tracks
L.L. Hill

Earth is crisscrossed by tracks, Otto thought as he nudged the bandaged navigation console to correct his course. Sparkles of nano particles left a bread crumb trail across a screen that led to Raquel.

Romans were great builders as they built on or across the tracks of people they conquered. Some ancient tracks were worn by the passage of many feet on their way to worship the procession of stars in stone circles. Planets, Earth, follow orbits with little deviation, yet no plotted course was ever the same across the void.

evacuation
last man had to fire
the escape pod

Mars Destiny
Richard E. Schell

When we met, little could we know where our fates and duties would take us or where our hearts would lead. We knew in advance what directions our paths might require.

When I look into the infinite night sky toward that distant red point of light, I comprehend the vastness of space that separates us. Yet when we speak, my heart waits impatiently longing for your eyes and voice in response.

Those are the times when twelve minutes become an eternity.

How different our lives might have been.

destined to be apart
without your touch
but forever bound to you

Synepeia ex machina
Richard E. Schell

You've been told everything. Why don't you believe me? I've worked here day and night for seven years, in general AI. I saw no harm in using it to make money trading the markets on my own time.

You've accused me of funding terrorism with the account. I knew nothing about it, even following the attack, when it profited greatly. I never contacted the politician with any trading advice or knew anything about blackmailing him after. Since then, the account was transferred, and I now have no access to any funds.

success requires a plan
but always anticipate
the unexpected

Lux Aeterna
Richard E. Schell

Militaristic ambitions and climate change expedited the collapse of once-sacred global boundaries beyond our expectations. The desires of mighty nations eclipsed the needs of the vulnerable, plunging the world into chaos. As unrest reigned, technology became a weapon and an oppressor.

Drones, minuscule as insects, proved instrumental in surveillance and warfare, leaving an indelible mark on humankind. An ominous social experiment spiraling beyond control, repercussions yet to be grasped.

Amidst the turmoil, humanity chose a new course. Technology becomes redirected to long-term growth and prosperity rather than a future of aggression and competition.

our nature betrays
technology redeems
morality renewed

Rabbit Moon
Richard E. Schell

There was no stopping Joan. She excelled at everything she ever tried. A brilliant student, a great athlete, beautiful and kind, she attended the best schools. She was now selected for the moon.

Joan always knew what she wanted. Even as a child, she claimed:" I'm going to the moon." With a Ph.D. in Physics, her dreams were coming true. But our daughter Janette was the joy of her life. The night before Joan's trip to space, she drew Janette's two pet rabbits on the moon. Then came that fateful day.

a shining life
cut short too soon
final legacy

Rabbits on the Moon
by Richard E. Schell

Fate's Unyielding Embrace
Richard E. Schell

When we met at the Mars colony, I knew you were not like the others. There was no way I could go through that again. Visiting you that day at work, seemed innocent enough. But I somehow sensed there was something between you two. One could see it by the way you looked into her eyes. We discussed it, yet my doubts persisted.

When I expelled you from the airlock, it was from love, not anger. I rejoiced, knowing our eventual reunion awaits, free from the imperfections of our mortal flaws.

fate's unyielding embrace
love eternally restored
in death's dominion

Straw of Sacrifice: Emissary's Dilemma
Richard E. Schell

Amidst interplanetary conflicts spanning several decades, we stood as Earth's chosen emissaries for the pivotal peace negotiations. As per our former foe's customs, the treaty's final signing was scheduled to coincide with an elaborate dinner. However, upon finishing the initial course, the foreign delegates abruptly insisted, "By partaking in our revered diplomat, your culture must reciprocate through the sacrifice of one of your peace ambassadors. This act shall symbolize faith and trust. Failure to comply will be seen by us as a grievous offense, rejecting our hard-fought accord."

in the name of duty
alien traditions dictated
drawing the fateful straw

Final Battle
Richard E. Schell

It was during the final battle of the Great Android War. Suspecting victory, we cautiously withdrew from our defensive position of safety. Suddenly I noticed him, one of the last droids left in the battle, battered beyond repair, with weapon sites directed at me. In his last moment, he intentionally lowered the gun and seemingly averted his gaze. Recognizing his condition, he then peacefully collapsed. It was as if he suddenly accepted his mortality and imminent demise. Like a final epiphany, a recognition of life's precious gift.

in our final fight
to save our humanity
did we not recognize theirs

Takes Two
Richard E. Schell

I write it off to boredom. Prep school just wasn't that challenging. Getting away with murder was another story.

Stephen was selected because he so needed to belong. After working on him for a while, he even believed he thought it up himself.

We overpowered Michael on his occasional nightly walk on the trail overlooking the lake. No one ever suspected anything happening to Michael other than an unfortunate fall. But no one ever figured out what happened to Stephan either, just as I planned it from the start.

two tasks are easier
when secrets are safest
kept by one

Echo of Deceit
Richard E. Schell

"In the news today, Chad Kincaid will be released in another twist in the Lakes serial murder case. If you recall, he was convicted two years ago for the eight murders in and around Lake County. He was found guilty based on extensive video surveillance and DNA evidence. In the last two months, however, there have been three more murders following the identical pattern, with the same calls to the police providing information only the killer could know."

"Thank you, brother, for picking me up and providing the perfect alibi for me."

times of need
loyalty runs deep
between twins

The Ambassador
Richard E. Schell

The Interplanetary Guild always had a diverse collection of attendees. None were more unusual than the ambassador from Pincoya. He had a sloth-like appearance and constantly carried around his cat-like pet, often to the discomfort of the other participants. It was made worse by that animal's constant interruptions.

When three Luytenian terrorists entered firing upon the assembly, they were dispatched by the ambassador himself, who bravely subdued them. In the battle, he sustained injuries protecting not only the delegation but that cat in particular. It made others suspect who the real Ambassador was.

best strategies
remain secret
in plain view

Casualties of the Interplanetary Colonial War
Richard E. Schell

I remember times spent playing with my brother and father as a child. That was before the decade-long Colonial War. Things changed so profoundly that I did not see Dad again until I was eighteen.

When he returned, he was a different person. Not just because his hands sometimes twitched uncontrollably. Or that he tried to conceal his scars earned in combat. It was the emotional wounds that weighed on his spirit.

Every once in a while, however, I see that rare smile or gesture of the man he always was.

victory's essence
lies not in battle
but conflicts endured

Illuminations of the Beyond
Richard E. Schell

In the late hours of the night, at that perfect time of the year when fall succumbs to inevitable winter, one can hear the wind whisper almost as if sentient voices were seeking your audience from a place beyond our comprehension. As you strain to hear and interpret these mysterious murmurs, you suddenly realize that you have crossed to where part of your being finds it nearly inconceivable that those calls could be anything other than real exchanges between conscious participants. Just as suddenly, you find yourself drifting back into wakefulness, did you not?

mysterious voices
dreams incarnate
realities grey

Luna est Zelotypus Amans: A Jealous Lover is the Moon
Richard E. Schell

Sarah was raised by her mother from the time she was three. She was always fascinated by space and her first memory was of her mother shooting off model rockets. Sarah never lost her interest in becoming an astronaut in the space program.

Eventually, her dream came true. After three missions to the moon, she got chosen to lead a six-month project. Problems arose around a month before her scheduled return, delaying her return for another six months. During this time her mother developed medical issues but didn't want to burden Sarah.

a year away
crowds cheer
mom's conspicuous absence

Ouija by Sandy DeLuca

Keeper – Logistics Base 415
Mark Jones

The war must be over. It's been twelve years since the other side probed this system and six since the last superluminal message. The message just said, Hold In Place. I get it, it's expensive to spin up messages to backwater rocks like this one.

So, I'm holding. Every day I do my training, 10k in full battle rattle. Then chow, then maintenance on the Mark IV Annihilators. Keeping entropy at bay, tending the graves, digging my own place for when the end comes. It might be soon.

in the bright graveyard
war machines rusting away
on low power mode

Thoughts and Dreams
Mark Jones

It is perfect! The body I didn't have at 18, flat stomach, firm breasts, toned and well muscled. The upgrades were worth every penny of two husbands' fortunes.

The memory transfer went well. Clone REM sleep is a good sign. Now all that is required is the consciousness transfer.

Voila! I'll have a new body to start another lifetime.

Glancing at her, the younger, not me, I see she is crying. Tears streak my younger face. Why is she crying? Are her dreams about my life?

my clone weeps alone
dreaming in her amniotic tank
fresh tears from old wounds

Last Meeting of Kings
Mark Jones

Flying low over the battlements the dragon lands gracefully in the city square. The beast is red and gold, crowned with golden horns on his huge head.

Housecarls draw weapons to defend their liege.

Then the dragon roars.

"Hold! I come to honor your lord!"

Mesmerized, the troops stand frozen.

The dragon approaches the bier. The dead king seems to be sleeping.

Gently caressing the king's scarred face with a maimed claw, the great beast whispers, "Honored adversary, worthy rival, beloved enemy, what times we had, you and I."

horned head bowed
the dragon grieves his foeman
weeping diamond tears

Counterattack
Benjamin Whitney Norris

The last one of its kind. Half-human, the anachronistic whelp. How implausible to have survived. Could there be a more insidious explanation? Following the invasion, the rebels wiped out in their stronghold by a biological weapon. They had no defense; or so it seemed. Down came the landing craft, then, with only the autonomous units left to turn the tide. And these so vulnerable to EMP. Their morale floundered on the plains, and they slithered underground. From their bunker under Sagamore Hill, they carried out earth's devastating counterattack.

kicking at the anthill
pus in boots
drained by a plasma lance

Harrowing Road
Benjamin Whitney Norris

Her husband of 25 years dropped dead of a heart attack on the kitchen floor. Beer from his last can foaming across the linoleum. The winning lotto numbers? Pinned to his blood-brain barrier by a shrike, with an icepick. Canned laughter. Their world coming apart at the seams. The fabric of reality but excuses drawn together on a loom, under the passage of a shuttle. Weaving the emperor's new clothes. Histories unraveled by the hour. The lies we tell when ashamed of ourselves, unable to wash the clay from our soles.

Harrowing Road
scours calluses and corns
cash crop humanity

Scorched Earth
Benjamin Whitney Norris

We're losing ground on the city streets. Get away if you can. Not the bridge! Take the tunnel under the river. Drones skim the rooftops taking potshots at those left behind: winged stool pigeons, invalids, die-hards... How we mourn for them! For their eulogies: subterranean passages from a book read by touch, kept out of sight. And those eyes in the sky? Blinded by visions of the coming apocalypse, an end of the world of their own making. They haul down the stars to scorch the countryside.

on a column of smoke
we rise up
hungering for dust and ashes

Word Made Flesh
Benjamin Whitney Norris

On the air: The word virus, typed out on a Burroughs adding machine. Numerology transmitted by wireless, playing $hell games with reality and the doors to perception. Thoughts bubbling up. Eggheads blown out by a phonographic needle. The scheming of our Saurian overlords? Flimsy as toilet paper under a pressure wash, the bidet of history. Today's gaslighting pop culture? Travelogues in a petri dish. A dirty old man off chasing skirts wakes up the next morning with a big goose egg... When nothing could be further from the truth.

the word made flesh
lying through her teeth
a rictus grin

Nativity
Greg Schwartz

After Earth, some of us settled on Mars. Others kept going, searching for new and distant worlds to inhabit, with varying degrees of success. Colonies sprouted and died, sparks of humanity blinking on and off across the galaxy like fireflies.

We tried to stay in touch with the others, tried to keep alive the shreds of tradition that we still had left. Even as we explored these strange new worlds, we clung to the old ways like a lifeline, a tether to our fading heritage. We knew if we let go, we'd be lost.

gas cloud
Santa's sleigh
rounds Jupiter

Grandma's Cookbook
Joy Yin

It was the weekend, and I had nothing to do, so I went to clean out my attic. I was going through some junk when I spotted Grandma's old cookbook. She'd passed years ago and had lived in a distant mansion in the countryside. She'd always seemed ... fishy. I'd caught her filling a bunch of holes in the yard and seen her add a berry-like thing into a pie. It didn't look like a strawberry. Curious, I flipped it open. The first recipe: Infant Heart Pie. I didn't dare read further.

found in attic
Grandma's cookbook
recipe: Infant Heart Pie

A Midsummer Night's Meal
Francis W. Alexander

Like Shakespeare, he compared her to a summer's day. She indeed appeared to be more lovely and temperate. After wooing her with a poem, he presented roses and a box of chocolates. Her meal was captivating.

"Will you be my valentine?" she said as she led him to her bed. Her tenderness mesmerized and her voice hypnotized him. Had she finally been the one to conquer this playboy? She slithered over him as if in a trance. He could not describe the unbearable delight. Sleep silenced his bliss.

early morning meal
there's never a good time
to meet a cannibal

When the Mushrooms Come
By Francis W. Alexander

The Atomic Age brought with it many wonders and great strides forward. It also brought nuclear war. We often forget how many nuclear warheads are still scattered about our world, and how many countries are still trying to make their own. What would happen to ordinary people if one fell without warning? Follow along in the lives of different people as they move through the drop of a nuclear bomb – before, during, and after the fall. See their lives before the flash, their reactions when the mushroom cloud rises, and how the survivors struggle on.

https://www.hiraethsffh.com/product-page/when-the-mushrooms-come-by-francis-w-alexander

A New Groove Move
Francis W. Alexander

Jay was my main road dog. Immensely talented, he could do the Moonwalk, Robot, Twist, and tap dance all in one move

Never, would I have imagined a real zombie apocalypse.

That fateful day, I had gone to his house. He shambled towards me. When I got to within three feet of him, I noticed the dark eyes and pale complexion.

"Brains," he said as he stared at me.

Although a zombie, he was trying to show me a new dance move before he was shot in the head.

bright sunny day –
showing kids how to do
the Jaywalk Slide

Poppers
Francis W. Alexander

FDA approved; Poppers hit the store shelves. Its price beat inflation because there was an unlimited supply of the seeds. You toss a handful into your mouth and enjoy crunching them. They burst in the mouth like popcorn releasing an odd captivating flavor. Despite the psychedelic out of body experience the seed was not dangerous.

Young and old were hooked on the food which had health benefits as well. Finding them was a miracle. Of course, there was a percentage of the population, the outliers, who did not eat the treats.

aliens
shedding some human organs and skin -
parasitism

Man of Perdition
Francis W. Alexander

His former cult members thrust darts of truth at him that fall like mist as he struts amongst the masses picking up new converts. No one could see the growing rash under his pinstripe suit. "He's a monster," his primary opponent warned. Not many listened.

Scorpio:
the snowflakes randomly forming
into a snowman

Under the red sky at night he, as their leader, struts throughout the land spreading skittles of peace. His primary opponent is now his most loyal follower. Blisters and barnacles tattoo his skin. His vomit of hate annihilates millions.

earth destroying asteroid:
answering a soul's
desperate prayer

Legend of the Iron Horse

(Homage to the song and image, Iron Horse by Jeff Christie 1972)

Marcia A. Borell

The great fear had swept across the bloody water. Too many people had died from the war and the illnesses that followed. Tracks were broken, food was scarce, and the mad kept fighting.

A whisper was spreading, crawling into ears as they collapsed into comas, 'the winged iron horse' was coming to save those that believed.

Made of iron and burnished steel, the thunderous clap of its beating wings screams through the night on sparking tracks or into the air over bomb-severed country.

Eternities clocks chime.

wings of iron flash

dying lips plead biting prayers

from their blood leeched graves

Skellies:
A Coloring Book
By Marcia A. Borell

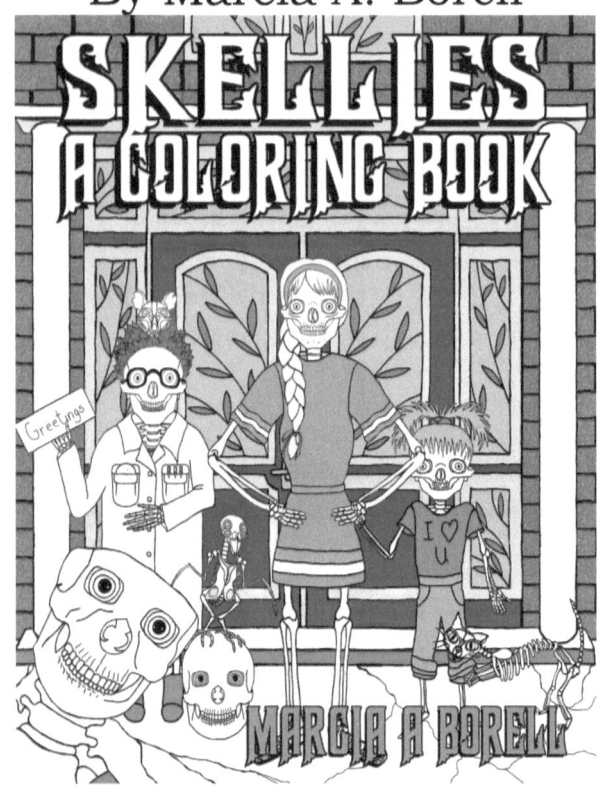

https://www.hiraethsffh.com/product-page/skellies-a-coloring-book-by-marcia-a-borell

The Bed
Marcia A. Borell

I can't sleep! This is my last hope! Of course, it would be made by Aliens, Inc. I broke my pledge to buy local. Anyway, it's arriving today. The ad said, "Sleep like you're floating on a cloud. Plug into any of the 100 dream sequences. We offer a lifetime guarantee." Does that mean they will send someone with a raygun if I don't sleep? It arrived with a team of short green aliens. They make high-pitched insect noises and don't blink as they watch me try to sleep.

clocks tick like thunder
somersaulting over the bed
vexed aliens weep

Tidings of Madness and Joy
The ABCs of the Great Old Ones

Greetings, Mortal! In these pages you will find tales of madness, see things beyond imagining, and you - yes YOU! - can bring them to life. Do you dare learn more about the Great Old Ones? Will you give them that which they crave? Or will you find yourself screaming as you learn absolute truth and see through the Great Beyond. Only time will tell. Come along and see what the Great Old Ones have to offer...

This is an incredibly unique coloring book and we are thrilled to finally be able to release it.

Get more dark and twisted tales with it and enjoy bringing the Old Gods to life in various ways.

https://www.hiraethsffh.com/product-page/tidings-of-madness-and-joy-by-marcia-borell-bill-otto

Understudies
By Priya Sridhar

The Stardust Sisters have always made their parody shows work. So what if they lost their third member to Hollywood? Does it even matter that they don't have a new theater facility? Grad school should fix that, twin sisters Stella and Evangeline calculate, and they'll get the funding, as well as a decent apartment in the city.

As if by miracle, an apartment with no rent opens up— in the Haunted Basilio Theater, where new management wants a fresh start after summer camp went wrong. All the twins have to do is perform a show scripted a century ago, and give up bits of their body heat. The show must go on, right? Right?!

Ordering Link:
Print Edition:
https://www.hiraethsffh.com/product-page/understudies-by-priya-sridhar
ePub Edition:
https://www.hiraethsffh.com/product-page/understudies-by-priya-sridhar-2
PDF edition:
https://www.hiraethsffh.com/product-page/understudies-by-priya-sridhar-1

Hairless Riddling Sphinx
Priya Sridhar

Her name is Beeswax, Bees for short. She rests her large head on my thighs and lays her butt firmly on my kneecaps, tail swishing back and forth. Sometimes she swats me if I fail to pet her.

Bees has no hair, because she is supposed to be hypoallergenic. She purrs riddles into my belly. She vibrates questions about what constantly rises every day and never goes down at the end of the day. Bees sometimes makes up riddles about birds and bugs she would like to eat.

    she makes wax puddles
    when irritated at me
    the best wood polish

Untitled
Terrie Leigh Relf

Even though it was just filled with books, a chair, and an overhead light, the spacious closet under the stairs was off-limits. It was strange how Auntie would spend hours reading there rather than in her comfy living room. She kept the door closed, and sometimes we could hear her reading out loud, which we thought was odd, but that was Auntie. What was odder still was when she finally opened the door and seemed so despondent. We were quite disturbed that her usual vibrant personality had been replaced by a shadow.

estate sale books
still possessed
by their owners

Untitled
Terrie Leigh Relf

It was a wonderful harvest celebration with all the village clothed in their best attire. The children appeared particularly happy traipsing through the fields, white helium balloons wound tightly 'round their wrists, pockets filled with candies and the last of autumn's fresh fruit. We cheered as the marching band circled 'round, announcing that the feast was about to begin. Giving thanks for this sumptuous meal, we looked skyward, knowing that winter would become cold and colder still, our fields soon barren. And then, the earth shifted, splitting open beneath our feet.

snowfall
how the chosen
were embraced by the sky

The Closet Under the Stairs
Terrie Leigh Relf

Even though it was just filled with books, a chair, and an overhead light, the spacious closet under the stairs was off limits. It was strange how Auntie would spend hours reading there rather than in a comfy living room chair. She kept the door closed, and sometimes we could hear her reading out loud, which we thought was odd. But that was Auntie. What was odder still was when she finally opened the door, she seemed so worn out, and rather than being her usually vibrant self, she seemed so sad.

estate sale books

still possessed

by their owners

The Sisterhood of the Blood Moon
By Terrie Leigh Relf

For thousands of Earth years, the Transgalactic Consortium has had an invested interest in this planet and its inhabitants, the Haurans. While the Sisterhood of the Blood Moon and the Guardians work together with the Consortium and Haurans to restore balance to the universe, the Blood Moon is fast approaching. The power of this moon reveals untold secrets . . . including the sacred covenant with the Mora Spiders. There is an ancient pact that continues to be honored - but at what cost and for whose purpose?

The world may come to an end. But will there be a chance for a new beginning? And if so, where?

https://www.hiraethsffh.com/product-page/sisterhood-of-the-blood-moon-by-terrie-leigh-relf

Why an Emergency Meeting of Boort's Trans-Galactic Astronomy Society Was Called
Terrie Leigh Relf

Dr. Suraj managed to remain composed as the Hauran astronomers viewed the five new stars on the screen. "This is quite spectacular," Dr. Collins repeated. "Why didn't we see them before?" Dr. Menaz wondered if there was a crack in the outer lens, while doctors Satterfield and Friedman calculated and recalculated their proximity. Meanwhile, *Boortean Survey Shuttle 7* conducted another sweep of the Atlantic Ocean's designated coordinates. Haura's supposedly anomalous black storm clouds were approaching active status. After the pilots confirmed their initial message to Boortean Command, they zip-zagged to safety.

optical illusion
to distract the Haurans
unauthorized portal activation

Untitled
Terrie Leigh Relf

Mara's dreams had been strange of late, then stranger still. This morning when she awoke, the last vestiges of one remained fresh within her memory. She recalled waves beginning to melt along the shore like blue-and-white plastic pieces beneath a broiling sun. Then night descended, and with it, yellow plastic stars emerged, shooting across the sky before freezing into place. But that wasn't the strangest part of the dream . . . It was the hands reaching down to pluck her off the beach to place her in a plastic box.

class project -
a child building a diorama
in their first dream walk

An Untoward Bliss of Moons
By Terrie Leigh Relf

It's her poetic tour de force. Nobody ever wrote poetry like this. Nobody else writes it now. Ms Relf not only takes the view from beyond the left field fence, she does it from a stadium in another galaxy. From "A Poet on Board" to "Why there are no poets on board" and "And so we set sail to Alpha Centauri," Ms Relf is at once poignant, amusing, acerbic, witty, charming, gauche, and sexy. In the universe of science fiction and fantasy poetry, she is nonpareil.

https://www.hiraethsffh.com/product-page/an-untoward-bliss-of-moons-by-terrie-leigh-relf

Announcing Steeple Gate High's Third Class Reunion
Terrie Leigh Relf

It was just like high school; more or less. You'd think that after The Conversion, personalities would change, behaviors would change, but no. Even the Unconverted, goody-two-shoes still behaved the same, whispering behind everyone's backs while they drank more than their fair share of the spiked Blood-Orange punch. I admit to being a bit bored until our former class president and current committee chairperson, Arturo, tapped on the mic and flashed his pearly-white fangs. We all gathered around him, curious and excited to discover what had been planned for this reunion's festivities.

full moon
the exquisite taste
of fresh blood

Untitled
Terrie Leigh Relf

As we journeyed toward Taran within the Shadowed Galaxy, communiques translated from many tongues warned us and others to avoid this area of space. We chose to ignore the rumors and innuendos, the lies and threats, the fairy tales and myths spun to dissuade us during this our final approach. We had no need or use for star charts and trans-galactic maps, pulled as we were by an unseen tether within our minds and hearts, pulled as we were by an invitation to descend, pulled as we were to follow our chosen course.

soft breeze
singing lullabies
by stasis cribs

Untitled
Terrie Leigh Relf

When the starslip's door opened, the team climbed through and paused to scan the strange, but somehow familiar, vista. Three silver moons had risen over the horizon. A bright-green river flowed down the mountain, depositing iridescent silt along its rocky banks. A school of some type of creature swam beneath delicate, golden seagrass. There were even bushes bowing beneath the weight of ripe purple fruit, which they tested before feasting upon. Venturing further down a narrow dirt path, they discovered a hot mineral spring, removed their gear, and gratefully immersed themselves.

upon awakening
still adrift in space
shared stasis dreams

Untitled
Terrie Leigh Relf

It had been several turns since Poda had experienced a good night's sleep. She yawned again, as much from boredom as exhaustion. While awaiting her turn to launch back to the orbital survey ship, the display screen streamed the usual odds-and-ends of ads: State-of-the-art living modules, domestic assistants, investment portfolios, solar sailing. None of the ads piqued her interest until an image of a bed appeared. "Sleepless days and nights? Experience our newest line of beds and mattresses imported from Selenia. Guaranteed to create blissful sleep no matter what quadrant you inhabit."

soothing music
an erotic presence
AI sleep chamber

Untitled
Terrie Leigh Relf

Once upon a time, there were zombies. Horrid creatures who devoured the flesh of their own kind, becoming something else, something other than human. Over the decades, zombies nearly decimated the human population until one day, they were just gone. Survivors began to emerge, cautious at first, and then with increased courage. Together, they began to rebuild abandoned towns and cities. Together, they began to procreate. Together, they began to research what had become of the zombies. We did what we could for mankind, but they are curious to a fault.

standing guard

at a subterranean lab

cryozenically-frozen zombie virus

The Last Good-Bye
-sakyu-

A hot summer day.

I walk to the playground alone. Time passes, and the shadows grow long as I sit on the bottom of the sliding board, the last heat of the day warming the shiny metal. My best friend is gone. Hit by a car while riding a bicycle.

Days are an eternity of idle loneliness for me, this one being no exception. A car drives by, some friends and their parents on the way home after a day at the pool. One of them gestures from the back window.

impossible sight
my dead friend waving
a last goodbye

Wrong Number
-sakyu-

The séance was over.

Madam Lilith's Reading Room was empty, the round table abandoned. The front windows with the purple neon "palms read" sign beckoned like the eyes of a skull.

Everyone had disappeared before the lights were even turned back on, the black cloth on the table left rustling in the sudden silence.

The group of grieving relatives had asked for a sign—any sign—that would prove that their dearly departed still existed on the Other Side. The sign they received had sent them all running.

melted candles
forming a six six six
the wrong spirit comes through

Those Who Die
by t.santitoro

A young nobleman's first sexual encounter is arranged by his father, to couple with a sentient plant being, a flauna-form. The youth unexpectedly falls in love with the plant/animal girl, and becomes totally addicted to her, fully knowing that—like the rest of her species—she only has one day to live.

When the object of his love at last roots herself to her home planet and becomes comatose for all eternity, the young man finds himself trapped in a state of incurable loss, unable to get her out of his mind.

Just by chance, he later discovers part of the flauna-form clinging to his clothes, and plants the leaf in his garden at home, tending a new version of flauna-form, hoping to one day find—and be reunited with—his lost beloved.

This is a story of tragedy, danger and moral decline, a Frankenstein-esque tale of creating that which threatens one's very existence.

https://www.hiraethsffh.com/product-page/those-who-die-by-t-santitoro

The Butler Did It
-sakyu-

Thunder rumbled overhead, rain pelting the score of black umbrellas, as mourners huddled around the grave, gathered into a knot like wet ravens, and the priest droned on. A woman stood alone by the cathedral's flying buttress, out of the torchlight, her straight-backed posture stiff, her gloved hand holding a handkerchief to her eyes as she sobbed beneath a black-veiled hat.

The deceased's widow caught sight of "the other woman", and gestured to the mechanized butler her husband had invented years ago. She had known about his affair all along.

settling a score
strong as an iron horse
mechanical assassin

The Only Option Left When Your Teeth Have Been Removed For Safety
-sakyu-

As I followed obediently behind, I watched my tiny master making her way down the sun-dappled glideway, totally unaware of the danger lurking ahead. I planted my six feet, refusing to continue, hoping to avoid what I perceived as an aggressive gang of alien thugs coming our way.

"Come on, Pinky," she coaxed, turning to urge me on, and thus putting her back to the approaching gang.

I trumpeted a warning, but she ignored my protest, tugging on my leash. There was nothing I could do to save my mistress!

the last resort
protecting my owner
by swallowing her whole

The Saint and the Demon
By t.santitoro & Ron Sparks

In the not-to-distant future, a young reporter reluctantly agrees to interview a senile old man in the heart of the Florida Everglades. In the humid, swampy environment, the reporter is sure that there can be no story of substance here, but the old man reveals that, in the past, his love was so strong and so passionate for a woman that he stopped at nothing to get her back when the forces of war tore them apart. He became a hero and a coward, a lover and a fighter . . . a saint and a devil. In his quest to rescue the woman he loved, he became something that she could no longer love.

Into the middle of this personal ordeal tumbles Cutter, a man from another world, sent to Earth to establish a breeding mission for his endangered race. He falls in love with an Earth woman, and must defend not only her, but also the future of his own people. The object of his alien affections, an innocent young woman named Angel, finds herself suddenly thrust into a world of aliens and intrigue, and of a love that has far more dangerous consequences than she could possibly have imagined.

Ordering Link:
Print: https://www.hiraethsffh.com/product-page/saint-and-the-demon-by-t-santitoro-and-ron-sparks
PDF: https://www.hiraethsffh.com/product-page/saint-the-demon-by-t-santitoro-ron-sparks
ePub: https://www.hiraethsffh.com/product-page/saint-amp-the-demon-by-t-santitoro-amp-ron-sparks

zombie drabbun
-sakyu-

Right next to the Bayou Cemetery, Momma Mirlande had a small voodoo shop where she sold trinkets and beads, but her attention was on a grave at the moment. She dug into the moist dirt, sweating and thinking. In life, Luc Pierre had treated Momma's daughter real bad. In death he had left her penniless. He'd died of an unmentionable disease, and she spat on his grave as she dug him up. Momma Mirlande was a bokor, and she'd fix him, alright. He'd be worse than dead.

charms and spells

uttering just the right words

he rises from the ground

The Way of Things
–sakyu–

Even comatose, Miani felt the suns warmth and the gentle morning rain of her home planet. She felt the life and energy of them coursing through her xylem and phloem. Two days ago, the TapRoot had blessed her union with an Arcturian. She now stood rooted in everlasting stupor, unsure whether the results of that coupling would be flora or fauna-form, but it didn't matter. She had mated and put down roots, connecting her to her world.

Her cranium suddenly burst open, revealing the largest flower her kind had ever known.

alien petals
a scented rainbow of hues
slowly unfurling

Still the Same
-sakyu-

"You're late."

I consulted my IPhone. It was only just after 7pm, so I was *not* late for the class reunion. I gave the werewolf and his zombie friend a raised eyebrow. "Sundown," I emphasized the word to make my point.

"Oh, yeah, right," said the zombie, shoving his elbow into the werewolf's side.

The hairy gent guffawed. He said, "Did you really aspire to these limitations before graduation? I mean, you were once voted Most Likely to Succeed."

"And *you* were voted Class Clown," I remarked, scoring another point.

three year reunion
most of the attendees
still the same

Dark Helmet (sorry, Spaceballs!)
-sakyu-

Korie met Sibastian in a space-station bar. He was tall, dark, handsome; every Terran girl's dream. She was a literal space virgin; he easily won her over with his charms, and his dark-purple eyes were disarmingly enchanting. They had spent three standard-days together on the station. She loved his coy way of letting her know he was horny.

"I'm--*hungry*," Sibastian growled into her ear in a suggestive manner.

So they passed the hours in the anti-grav well, locked in the limbo of foreplay, until the moment she finally gave in.

penetration

digesting her from the inside

his other head

Adopted Child
By Teri Santitoro

Imp, now 13, has awakened from stasis by MA, the ship's computer, to find that everyone else has been killed by a highly infectious disease. She is alone on the ship. But she is about to have visitors.

The *Greentown*, a salvage ship, has spotted a derelict and is about to board her for salvage rights. The crew is blissfully unaware of what happened to the people on the derelict. Soon enough they will find out...but will it be too late? And what of the girl who now controls the derelict?

To everyone involved, everything is new...and potentially lethal.

https://www.hiraethsffh.com/product-page/adopted-child-by-t-santitoro

Bee's Knees
-sakyu-

The first examples of alien life-forms appeared following examinations of a crashed vessel of unknown origin. Biologists were puzzled by the fuzzy creatures buzzing skyward in a cloud that quickly dissipated into thin air.

Reported sightings overwhelmed our scientists, but those sightings began to change, like the creatures themselves. At first the alien organisms hovered over the inverted plant-cups which filled our agricultural fields. They congregated among the colorful cups, but no one understood why. Finally, the miniscule creatures began to clutch onto the plant-cups, their legs seemingly mutated to grasp the delicate under-parts.

alien life-forms
mutated
surviving and thriving

Never Look a Gift Landwayl in the Nose

-sakyu-

The balihickle shook from side to side with each step the gigantic landwayl took, and inside the shaded cabin, the five tourists were thrown about, eliciting surprised grunts as they bumped against one another.

"I say," said an older gent from Terra. "I never imagined myself traveling by landwayl!"

"With good reason," groused another passenger. "This isn't the most comfortable means of reaching Comsteekton!"

"Balihickles are quaint" the first man argued. "And the price was included in my travel-package!"

"Hey, I had to pay extra!" complained someone else.

ponderous foot falls
the dust cloud billows higher
choking on the upgrades

Who?

Francis Wesley Alexander: If you don't see Wes stuffing his mouth with macaroni and cheese, or pulling a cord; you can believe he is writing.

Linette Marie Allen, winner of the 2021 Kay Murphy Prize for Poetry, holds an MFA in Creative Writing and the Publishing Arts from the University of Baltimore. A Turner Fellow, she has published work in journals worldwide, including Pleiades, Gulf Coast, and Prairie Schooner. Twice nominated for the Best of the Net Awards, her writing was set to music by composers at The Peabody Institute. When not writing, she is sketching in charcoal: mushrooms, mice under moonlight, the mountains.

Randall Andrews is an award-winning fiction writer and poet from southern Michigan. When not writing, he can be found wearing the soles off a pair of running shoes, listening to his favorite John Williams soundtracks, or hand-feeding his loyal flock of wild songbirds.

Roxanne Barbour is a writer from Burnaby, BC, Canada. She has written numerous novels: *An Alien Collective*; *Revolutions*; *Sacred Trust*; *Kaiku*; *Alien Innkeeper*; *An Alien Confluence*; *Alien Innkeeper on Particle*. She also writes speculative poetry, and has published in *Scifaikuest, Star*Line, Polar Borealis, Polar Starlight*, *Dwarf Stars,* and many other magazines.

H.T. Grossen lives and writes beneath the long evening shadow of the Rocky Mountains in Pueblo, Colorado with his magical wife and pulchritudinous daughters. He writes poems and fiction of many genres, mainly Science Fiction and Fantasy. htgrossen.com

Terrie Leigh Relf is on staff at Hiraeth Publishing and *Tales from the Moonlit Path*. In addition to being a writer and editor, she also teaches for National University and is a writing and live coach.

-sakyu- is the poetry pen name of **t. santitoro**, on staff at Hiraeth Publishing as the editor of *Scifaikuest,* and author of several novels including *The Saint and the Demon* (with **Ron Sparks**), *The Legend of Trey Valentine, Those Who Die* and *Adopted Child.*

Richard E. Schell works in the biomedical field in California. He enjoys writing and has been published over fifty times in both the biomedical field as well as in fictional genres and poetry. He enjoys photography, literature, and travel. He also volunteers in animal rescue.

Joy Yin is a writer, poet, and artist from Wuhan, China, though she has lived in California for 5 years. She is fluent in Mandarin and English but also learning Spanish. Joy has always had a love for reading and writing. As of now, she has works either forthcoming or already published in Skipping Stones Magazine, Scfaikuest, the new Drabbun Anthology (Hiraeth Books), Cold Moon Journal, Triya, Star*Line, and more. She's currently 13 years old and attending an international school in Mexico City. Right now, she's working on a collection of micro-poetry. In her free time, she likes to curl up and read a good book (however, she doesn't quite like rereading). Find her on Instagram at @joyyinm88.

Lee Clark Zumpe, an entertainment editor with Tampa Bay Newspapers, earned his bachelor's in English at the University of South Florida. He began writing poetry and fiction in the early 1990s. His work has regularly appeared in a variety of literary journals and genre magazines over the last two decades. Publication credits include Tiferet, Zillah, The Ugly Tree, Modern Drunkard Magazine, Red Owl, Jones Av., Main Street Rag, Space & Time, Mythic Delirium and Weird Tales. Lee lives on the west coast of Florida with his wife and daughter.

www.ingramcontent.com/pod-product-compliance
Lightning Source LLC
LaVergne TN
LVHW092052060526
838201LV00047B/1360